For:

From:

Date:

Brownlow Publishing Company
6309 Airport Freeway
Fort Worth, Texas 76117

ISBN: 1-57051-029-6

Cover/interior:
Koechel Peterson & Associates

Printed in Singapore

All Things Great & Small

Brownlow

Brownlow Publishing Company, Inc.

Little Treasures Miniature Books

A Little Cup of Tea

All Things Great & Small

Angels of Friendship

Baby's First Little Bible

Cherished Bible Stories

Dear Teacher

Faith

For My Secret Pal

From Friend to Friend

Grandmothers Are for Loving

Hope

Love

Mother

My Sister, My Friend

Precious Are the Promises

Quilted Hearts

Soft as the Voice of an Angel

The Night the Angels Sang

Greatness is a matter,
not of size, but of quality,
and it is within the reach of
every one of us. Greatness lies
in the faithful performance
of whatever duties life
places upon us and in the
generous performance of the
small acts of kindness that
God has made possible for us.

SIDNEY GREENBERG

If I cannot
do great things,
I can do
small things
in a great way.
JAMES FREEMAN CLARKE

Since we have loaves, let us not look for cakes.

SPANISH PROVERB

Where'er I am,

by shore,

at sea,

I think of thee.

DAVID M. MOIR

He Set You There

Is your place a small place?

Tend it with care!—

He set you there.

Is your place a large place?

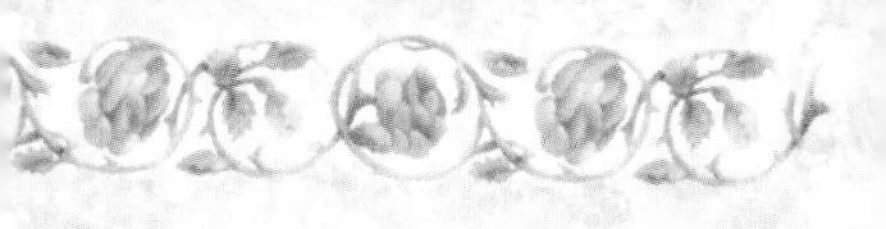

Guard it with care!—

He set you there.

Whate'er your place, it is

Not yours alone, but His

Who set you there.

JOHN OXENHAM

The happiest moments
my heart knows
are those
in which it is
pouring forth
its affections to
a few esteemed
characters.

THOMAS JEFFERSON

Friendship flourishes at the fountain of forgiveness.

WILLIAM ARTHUR WARD

Don't lead me;

I may not follow.

Don't walk behind me,

I may not lead.

Walk beside me

and be my friend.

ANONYMOUS

True Greatness

The beginning of greatness
is to be little;
the increase of greatness
is to be less;
the perfection of greatness
is to be nothing.

DWIGHT LYMAN MOODY

Small Charities

The happiness of life is made
up of minute fractions—
the little, soon forgotten
charities of a kiss or smile,
a kind look, a heartfelt
compliment, and the
countless infinitesimals of
pleasurable and genial feeling.

SAMUEL TAYLOR COLERIDGE

Children are
God's apostles,
day by day
sent forth to
preach of love,
and hope,
and peace.

JAMES RUSSELL LOWELL

That which is
striking and beautiful
is not always good,
but that which
is good is
always beautiful.

NINON DE L'ENCLOS

The Way to Happiness—

Keep your heart

free from hate,

your mind from worry,

live simply, expect little,

give much.

ANONYMOUS

Two souls

with but a

single thought,

Two hearts

that beat

as one.

VON MÜNCH BELLINGHAUSEN

What do we live for,
if it is not to make
life less difficult
to each other?

GEORGE ELIOT

Friendship is
in loving
rather than in
being loved.

ROBERT SEYMOUR BRIDGES

I Said a Prayer for You Today

I said a prayer
for you today
And know God
must have heard;
I felt the answer
in my heart
Although He spoke
not a word.

I asked for
happiness for you
in all things
great and small,
But that you'd know
His loving care
I prayed the most of all.

AUTHOR UNKNOWN

Whatever one possesses becomes of double value, when we have the opportunity of sharing it with others.

BOUILLY

If we are
truly prudent
we shall cherish
those noblest
and happiest of
our tendencies—
to love and
to confide.

EDWARD BULWER-LYTTON

The

sweetest music

isn't in oratorios,

but in kind words.

RALPH WALDO EMERSON

Anyone with a
heart full of
friendship has
a hard time
finding enemies.

ANONYMOUS

Never fear spoiling children by making them too happy. Happiness is the atmosphere in which all good affections grow.

BRAY

Contentment is not
the fulfillment of
what you want,
but the realization
of how much
you already have.

Fountain of Joy

Happiness is caused by things that happen around me, and circumstances will mar it; but joy flows right on through trouble; joy flows on through the dark; joy flows in the night as well

as in the day; joy flows all through persecution and opposition. It is an unceasing fountain bubbling up in the heart; a secret spring the world can't see and doesn't know anything about.

DWIGHT LYMAN MOODY

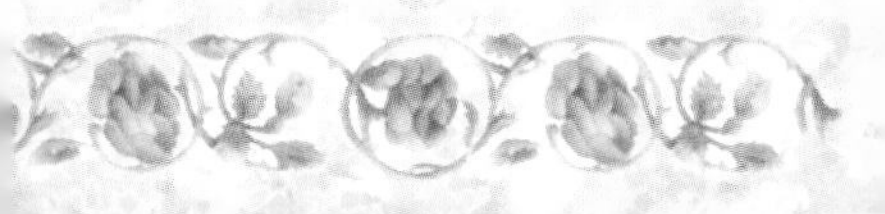

True Riches

Some have much,
and some have more,
Some are rich,
and some are poor,
Some have little,
some have less,
Some have not a cent to bless;
Their empty pockets yet possess
True riches in true happiness.

JOHN OXENHAM

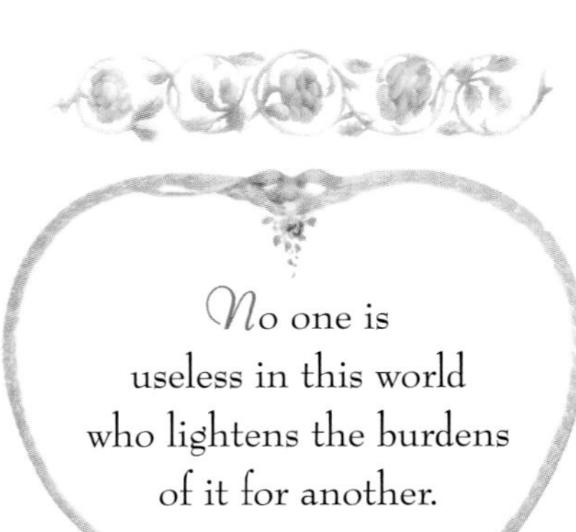

No one is
useless in this world
who lightens the burdens
of it for another.

CHARLES DICKENS

The great man
is he who
does not lose
his child's heart.
MENG-TZU

Be a friend.
You don't need glory.
Friendship is a simple story.
Pass by trifling errors blindly,
Gaze on honest effort kindly,
Cheer the youth
who's bravely trying,
Pity him who's sadly sighing;
Just a little labor spend
On the duties of a friend.

EDGAR A. GUEST

Servant of All

Whoever wants to
become great among you
must be your servant,
and whoever wants to be
first must be servant of all.
For even the Son of Man
did not come to be served,
but to serve.

MARK 10:43-45

Kindness

Kindness in words
creates confidence.
Kindness in thinking
creates profoundness.
Kindness in giving
creates love.

LAO-TSE

The world is so empty
if one thinks only
of mountains, rivers,
and cities; but to
know someone who
thinks and feels with
us in spirit, this makes
the earth for us an
inhabited garden.

JOHANN WOLFGANG VON GOETHE

Large streams
from little
fountains flow,
Tall oaks
from little
acorns grow.

DAVID EVERETT

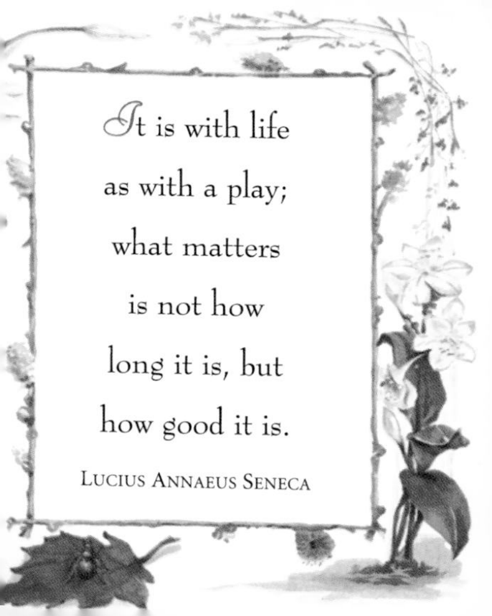

It is with life
as with a play;
what matters
is not how
long it is, but
how good it is.

LUCIUS ANNAEUS SENECA

Flowers of Love

Bright flowers shall
bloom wherever we rove,
A voice divine shall
talk in each stream;
The stars shall look
like worlds of love,
and this earth be
all one beautiful stream.

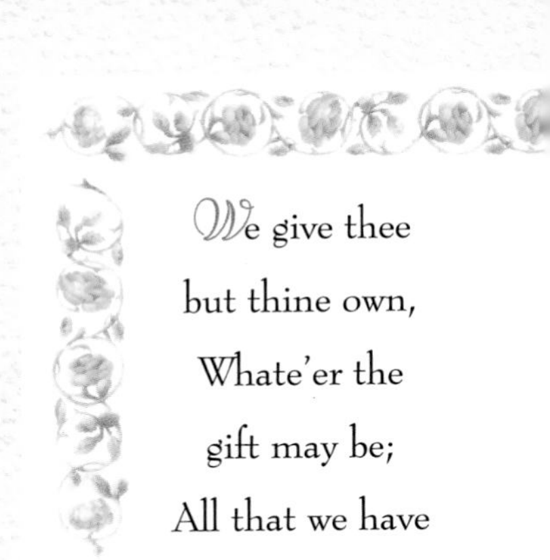

We give thee
but thine own,
Whate'er the
gift may be;
All that we have

is thine alone,

A trust,

O Lord,

from thee.

WILLIAM WALSHAM HOW

He Prayeth Best

He prayeth best
who loveth best
All things both
great and small;
For the dear God
who loveth us,
He made and loveth all.

SAMUEL TAYLOR COLERIDGE

Great works do not
always lie in our way,
but every moment
we may do little ones
excellently, that is,
with great love.

SAINT FRANCIS OF SALES

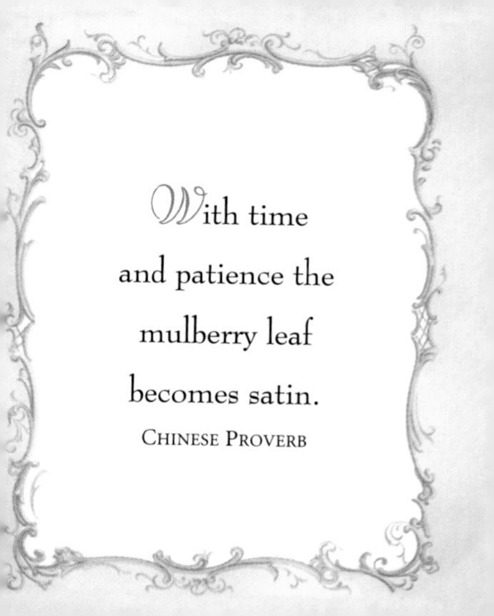

With time
and patience the
mulberry leaf
becomes satin.

CHINESE PROVERB

Friendship is a spiritual thing.
It is independent of matter
or space or time. That which
I love in my friend is not
that which I see.
What influences me
in my friend is not
his body, but his spirit.

JOHN DRUMMOND

Life is short and we have not too much time for gladdening the hearts of those who are traveling the dark way with us. Oh, be swift to love! Make haste to be kind!

HENRI FREDERIC AMIEL

Part of the Chorus

It is not required of
every man and woman
to be or to do
something great;

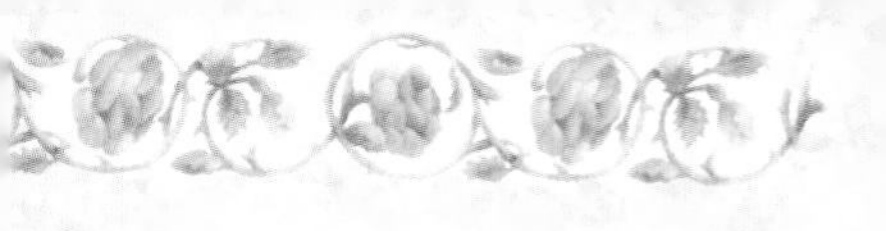

most of us must
content ourselves with
taking small parts in
the chorus, as far as
possible without discord.

HENRY VAN DYKE

There are two ways

of spreading light:

to be the candle

or the mirror

that reflects it.

EDITH WHARTON

You give but little
when you give of
your possessions.
It is when you give
of yourself that
you truly give.

KAHLIL GIBRAN

No man can tell
whether he is rich
or poor by turning
to his ledger. It is
the heart that
makes a man rich.

HENRY WARD BEECHER

How dear

to this heart

are the scenes

of my childhood,

when fond recollection

presents them to view!

SAMUEL WOODWORTH

Little Things

I thank Thee for
a daily task to do,
For books that are my
ships with golden wings.
For mighty gifts let
others offer praise—
Lord, I am thanking
Thee for little things.

If the

world is cold,

make it

your business

to build fires.

HORACE TRAUBEL

Do little
things now;
so shall big things
come to thee
by and by
asking to
be done.

PERSIAN PROVERB

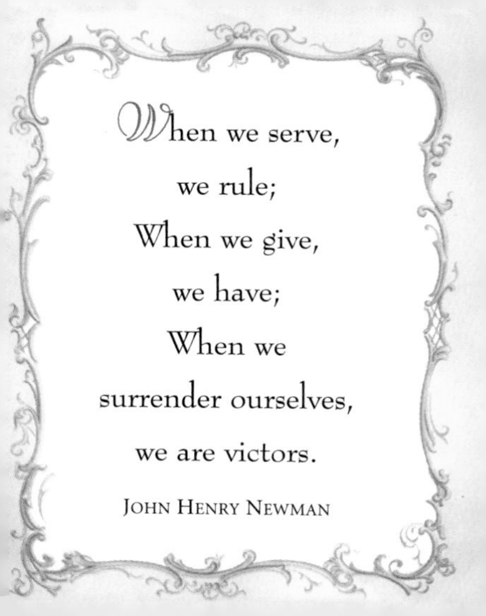

When we serve,
we rule;
When we give,
we have;
When we
surrender ourselves,
we are victors.

JOHN HENRY NEWMAN

Make a rule and pray to God
to help you to keep it, never,
if possible, to lie down at night
without being able to say:
"I have made one human being
at least a little wiser, or
a little happier, or at least
a little better this day."

CHARLES KINGSLEY

He who wants little always has enough.

JOHANN GEORG ZIMMERMAN

That best portion of
a good man's life,
His little, nameless,
unremembered acts
Of kindness and love.

WILLIAM WORDSWORTH

Little Cakes

We can do little things
for God: I turn the cake that
is frying on the pan, for love
of Him; and that done, if
there is nothing else to call me,
I bow in worship before Him
who has given me grace
to work; afterwards I rise
happier than a king.

BROTHER LAWRENCE

A great man shows
his greatness by the way
he treats little men.

THOMAS CARLYLE

When it comes to life,
the critical thing is whether
you take things for granted
or take them with gratitude.

G. K. CHESTERTON

The best and
most beautiful things
in the world
cannot be seen
or even touched.
They must be felt
with the heart.

JOHANN WOLFGANG VON GOETHE

It is goodness,
not greatness,
that will do you good.

ANONYMOUS

He who is
plenteously provided
for from within needs
but little from without.

JOHANN WOLFGANG VON GOETHE

Little Words of Love

Little drops of water,
little grains of sand,
Make the mighty ocean
and the pleasant land.
Little deeds of kindness,
little words of love,
Help to make earth happy
like the heaven above.

JULIA A. FLETCHER CARNEY

Nothing is more simple
than greatness; indeed,
to be simple is to be great.

RALPH WALDO EMERSON

Our business is not to
see what lies dimly
at a distance, but to do
what lies clearly at hand.

THOMAS CARLYLE

Kind words toward
those you daily meet,
kind words and actions
right, will make this life
of ours most sweet,
turn darkness into light.

ISAAC WATTS

Great events,
we often find,
On little things depend,
And even small beginnings
Have oft a mighty end.

UNKNOWN

The greatest truths
are the simplest, and so
are the greatest men.

AUGUST W. HARE

Those who wish
to sing always
find a song.

SWEDISH PROVERB

Love in Action

Goodness is love in action,
love with its hand to the plow,
love with the burden on
its back, love following
his footsteps who went about
continually doing good.

JAMES HAMILTON

The princes

among us

are those who

forget themselves

and serve

mankind.

WOODROW WILSON

Blessed is the influence of one true, loving human soul on another.

GEORGE ELIOT

Goodness consists
not in the outward
things we do,
but in the inward
thing we are.

Edwin Hubbel Chapin